See It Grow
CRANBERRY

by Jackie Lee

Consultant: Karen C. Hall, PhD
Applied Ecologist, Botanical Research Institute of Texas
Fort Worth, Texas

BEARPORT
PUBLISHING

New York, New York

Credits

Title Page, © Dionisvera/Shutterstock; TOC, © Muskoka Stock Photos/Shutterstock; 4, © ValentinaProskurina/Shutterstock; 5T, © Brent Hofacker/Shutterstock; 5B, © MoonRaiter/Shutterstock; 6, © Madlen/Shutterstock; 7, © Tyler W. Smith; 8, © Nordroden/Shutterstock; 9, © 2015 Evergreen Nursery Company Inc; 10–11, © Julie Feinstein/Dreamstime; 11, © Enskanto/iStock; 12T, © UMass Cranberry Station, Wareham, Mass.; 12B, © Robert Biedermann/Shutterstock; 13, © Madlen/Shutterstock; 14, © david olah/iStock; 15, © mikute/Shutterstock; 16–17, © Xuanlu Wang/Shutterstock; 18, © Kevin Miller/iStock; 19, © Richard Cavalleri/Shutterstock; 20, © Zigzag Mountain Art/Shutterstock; 21, © ligora/Thinkstock; 22, © Muskoka Stock Photos/Shutterstock; 22T, © Potapov Alexander/Shutterstock; 22B, © Madlen/Shutterstock; 23 (T to B), © KevinMiller/iStock, © Madlen/Shutterstock, © david olah/iStock, © David Tadevosian/Shutterstock, © Hong Vo/Shutterstock, and © mikute/Shutterstock; 24, © Dionisvera/Shutterstock.

Publisher: Kenn Goin
Editorial Director: Natalie Lunis
Senior Editor: Joyce Tavolacci
Creative Director: Spencer Brinker
Design: Debrah Kaiser
Photo Researcher: Olympia Shannon

Library of Congress Cataloging-in-Publication Data

Lee, Jackie, active 2015, author.
  Cranberry / by Jackie Lee.
      pages cm. — (See it grow)
  Summary: "In this book, readers will learn how cranberries grow" — Provided by publisher.
  Audience: Ages 4–8.
  Includes bibliographical references and index.
  ISBN 978-1-62724-841-9 (library binding) — ISBN 1-62724-841-2 (library binding)
  1. Cranberries—Juvenile literature. I. Title. II. Series: See it grow.
  QK495.E68L44 2016
  634.76—dc23
                              2015013382

For more information, write to Bearport Publishing Company, Inc., 45 West 21st Street, Suite 3B, New York, New York 10010. Printed in the United States of America.

10 9 8 7 6 5 4 3 2 1

Contents

Cranberry 4

Cranberry Facts 22

Glossary 23

Index 24

Read More 24

Learn More Online 24

About the Author 24

Cranberry

Cranberries are tiny, **tart** fruits.

They are smooth, round, and red.

How did they get that way?

Cranberries can be made into sauce. The sauce is often eaten on Thanksgiving. Cranberries are also used to make muffins and juice.

Every cranberry plant starts out as a tiny seed.

After the seed is planted, it starts to grow.

seed

Tiny roots form underground.

A green **shoot** pushes up through the soil.

shoot

Roots take in water and **nutrients** from the soil.

Soon, the shoot grows into a little plant.

It has a stem and many leaves.

stem

Cranberry leaves stay green all year long.

The cranberry plant gets bigger.

It becomes a **vine**.

The vine spreads out along the ground.

vine

Many vines grow together in places called bogs.

Bogs have wet, soggy soil.

cranberry bog

The state with the most cranberry bogs is Wisconsin.

11

After about
two years,
flower buds
form on the vine.

buds

Soon, the
buds open.

flower

The flowers are pink and white.

In a few weeks, the flowers turn into cranberries.

At first, the berries are pale green.

Then, as they **ripen**, they turn red.

The ripe berries have a tart taste.

It's time to **harvest** the berries!

Farmers flood the bog.

The berries are harvested in fall.

Next, the farmers use a machine called a beater.

It knocks the berries off the vines.

The berries float to the top of the water.

The farmers gather them.

Why do cranberries float? They are filled with tiny pockets of air.

Most of the berries will be eaten.

However, some will be used for the seeds inside.

The seeds will grow into new vines!

Cranberry Facts

- Native Americans used cranberries for food, fabric dyes, and medicine.

- One-fifth of all the cranberries harvested each year are eaten on Thanksgiving.

- At first, cranberries were called *craneberries*. That's because the flowers look like the heads of large waterbirds called cranes.

- Because cranberries are filled with air, they bounce.

Glossary

 **harvest** (HAR-vist) to gather ripe fruit

 nutrients (NOO-tree-uhnts) substances that plants get from the soil, which they need to grow and be healthy

 **ripen** (RYE-pin) to become fully grown and ready for eating

 **shoot** (SHOOT) a young plant that has just appeared above the soil

tart (TART) sour in flavor

 vine (VINE) a plant that grows along the ground

Index

berries 14–15, 18–19, 20–21

bogs 11, 16–17

flowers 12–13, 14, 22

food 5, 22

harvesting 16–17, 18–19

nutrients 7

roots 7

seeds 6, 21

shoot 7, 8

soil 7, 11

Thanksgiving 5, 22

vine 10–11, 18, 21

Read More

LaPenta, Marilyn. *Fall Shakes to Harvest Bakes (Yummy Tummy Recipes: Seasons)*. New York: Bearport (2013).

Snyder, Inez. *Cranberries (Welcome Books)*. New York: Scholastic (2004).

Learn More Online

To learn more about cranberries, visit
www.bearportpublishing.com/SeeItGrow

About the Author

Jackie Lee lives in upstate New York and enjoys cooking and baking with ripe, red cranberries.